TOP 10 MOMENTS IN HOCKEY

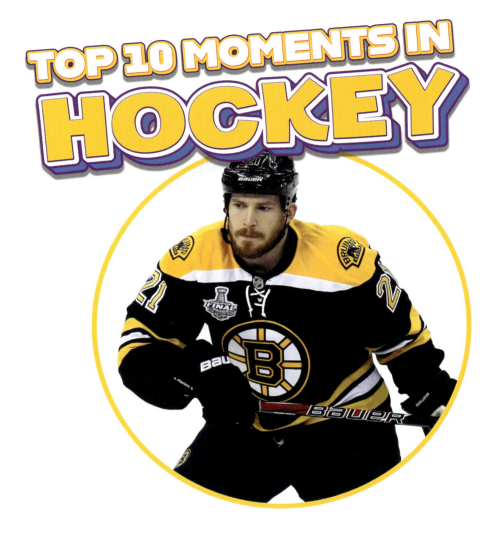

BY NATHAN SOMMER

Minneapolis, Minnesota

Credits

Cover and title page, © Anthony Nesmith/Associated Press and © johnalexandr/Adobe Stock and © vchalup/Adobe Stock; 4, © SergejsKuznecovs/Adobe Stock and © shock/Adobe Stock and © Andrii Iurlov/Adobe Stock and © robert decelis/ Adobe Stock and © bernardbodo/Adobe Stock and © Ruslan Shevchenko/Adobe Stock and © Vladislav Gajic/Adobe Stock and © Marko Hannula/Adobe Stock and © Gorodenkoff Productions OU/Adobe Stock and © Gorodenkoff/Adobe Stock and © modestil/Adobe Stock and © Ross Bonander/Adobe Stock and © Inna Darda/Adobe Stock and © dusan petkovic/ Adobe Stock and © Pavel Kašák/Adobe Stock and © Losevsky Pavel/Adobe Stock and © Anna Stakhiv/Adobe Stock and © master1305/Adobe Stock and © Robert Nyholm propic.se/Adobe Stock and © Sergey Novikov/Adobe Stock and © diy13/ Adobe Stock and © johnalexandr/Adobe Stock and © Cavan/Adobe Stock and © 103tnn/Adobe Stock and © Andrey Baturin/Adobe Stock and © BerkahStock/Adobe Stock; 5, © Focus On Sport/Getty Images; 6, © The Washington Post/Getty Images; 6–7, © John Locher/Associated Press; 8, © Bob Jordan/Associated Press; 9, © Ron Frehm/Associated Press; 10–11, © Doug Pizac/Associated Press; 12, © B Bennett/Getty Images; 13, © Eric Draper/Associated Press; 14–15, © Brian Babineau/ Getty Images; 15, © Steve Babineau/Getty Images; 16, © Zuma Press, Inc./Alamy Stock Photo; 17, © Houston Chronicle/ Hearst Newspapers/Getty Images; 18, © Associated Press; 18–19, © Heinz Kluetmeier/Getty Images; 20, © Associated Press; 20–21, © A.E. Maloof/Associated Press; 22TR, © Alan Diaz/Associated Press; 22ML, © B Bennett/Getty Images; 22BR, © Lee Balterman/Getty Images; 23BR, © BillionPhotos/Adobe Stock

Bearport Publishing Company Product Development Team

Publisher: Jen Jenson; Director of Product Development: Spencer Brinker; Editorial Director: Allison Juda; Editor: Cole Nelson; Editor: Tiana Tran; Production Editor: Naomi Reich; Art Director: Kim Jones; Designer: Kayla Eggert; Designer: Steve Scheluchin; Production Specialist: Owen Hamlin

Statement on Usage of Generative Artificial Intelligence

Bearport Publishing remains committed to publishing high-quality nonfiction books. Therefore, we restrict the use of generative AI to ensure accuracy of all text and visual components pertaining to a book's subject. See BearportPublishing.com for details.

Library of Congress Cataloging-in-Publication Data is available at www.loc.gov or upon request from the publisher.

ISBN: 979-8-89577-065-8 (hardcover)
ISBN: 979-8-89577-512-7 (paperback)
ISBN: 979-8-89577-182-2 (ebook)

Copyright © 2026 Bearport Publishing Company. All rights reserved. No part of this publication may be reproduced in whole or in part, stored in any retrieval system, or transmitted in any form or by any means, electronic, mechanical, photocopying, recording, or otherwise, without written permission from the publisher. Bearport Publishing is a division of FlutterBee Education Group.

For more information, write to Bearport Publishing, 3500 American Blvd W, Suite 150, Bloomington, MN 55431.

CONTENTS

The Fastest Team Sport 4

#10 Five Goals, Five Ways 5

#9 Winning the Title 6

#8 Messier's Guarantee 8

#7 The Miracle on Manchester 10

#6 Montreal's Fifth Straight 12

#5 Gretzky Makes History 13

#4 The Bruins Bounce Back 14

#3 The Golden Goal 16

#2 The Miracle on Ice 18

#1 The Flying Goal 20

Even More Extreme Hockey Moments 22

Glossary. 23

Index 24

Read More. 24

Learn More Online 24

About the Author 24

THE FASTEST TEAM SPORT

Hockey is a thrilling, fast-paced sport. Olympic and National Hockey League (NHL) games have wowed fans with their speedy action, amazing goals, and surprising comebacks.

WHAT ARE THE TOP 10 MOMENTS IN HOCKEY?

Read on to decide for yourself. . . .

#10 FIVE GOALS, FIVE WAYS

December 31, 1988 ▪ Pittsburgh Civic Arena ▪ Pittsburgh, Pennsylvania

Pittsburgh Penguins **center** Mario Lemieux ended 1988 on a high. During his game against the New Jersey Devils, he scored five goals in five different ways! In the first period, Lemieux scored an **even-strength goal**, a **short-handed goal**, and a **power-play goal**. Then, he hit a **penalty shot** in the second, and an **empty-net goal** in the third.

Lemieux scored his first 3 goals within the first 10 minutes of the game.

The Penguins went on to defeat the Devils 8–6.

Lemieux was voted MVP for the 1988–1989 season.

Lemieux in 1988

5

#9 WINNING THE TITLE

June 7, 2018 ▪ T-Mobile Arena ▪ Las Vegas, Nevada

Alexander Ovechkin is one of the greatest hockey players of all time. But during his first 12 seasons with the Washington Capitals, the team didn't win a single championship. That changed during Game 5 of the 2018 Stanley Cup. Ovechkin led the Capitals to a 4–3 victory, coming back from behind against the Vegas Golden Knights!

Ovechkin was MVP of the 2018 Stanley Cup playoffs.

The Golden Knights entered this series as the favorites to win.

During the 2017–2018 season, Ovechkin led the NHL in scoring with 49 goals.

Ovechkin is 1 of only 3 players in NHL history to score more than 800 goals.

This was only the second time the Capitals had played in the Stanley Cup.

Ovechkin tries to shoot past Golden Knights goalie Marc-André Fleury.

#8 MESSIER'S GUARANTEE

May 25, 1994 ▪ Brendan Byrne Arena ▪ East Rutherford, New Jersey

After 5 games, the New York Rangers trailed the New Jersey Devils 3–2 in the 1994 Eastern Conference finals. But Rangers captain Mark Messier was determined to turn things around. He promised reporters a Game 6 victory—and he delivered. The Devils led 2–1 late in the game. Then, Messier scored a **hat trick** and took over the win.

The Rangers went on to win the 1994 Stanley Cup. This was their first championship in 54 years.

The Rangers celebrate their 1994 Stanley Cup win.

#7 THE MIRACLE ON MANCHESTER

April 10, 1982 • The Forum • Inglewood, California

In Game 3 of the 1982 Stanley Cup playoffs' first round, the Los Angeles Kings trailed the Edmonton Oilers 5–0. Scoreless before the third period, a Kings comeback seemed impossible. However, the Kings scored five goals in a row—the last shot with only five seconds left! Then, Kings player Daryl Evans earned the win with a **slap shot** in overtime.

The Kings won the series in Game 5.

During the 1981–1982 season, the Oilers had scored 103 more goals than the Kings.

This game is called Miracle on Manchester because it was played at The Forum, which was located on Manchester Boulevard.

This game was the biggest comeback in NHL playoff history.

The Kings entered the playoffs this season as underdogs.

Oilers player Jari Kurri *(center)* and Kings player Steve Bozek *(right)* battling for the puck

#6 MONTREAL'S FIFTH STRAIGHT

April 14, 1960 • Maple Leaf Gardens • Toronto, Ontario

The Montreal Canadiens crushed the Toronto Maple Leafs in the 1960 Stanley Cup. Across the series, they outscored the Leafs 15–5 to win every game. The victory was the Canadiens fifth championship win in a row. This is an NHL record that stands to this day! It is thought of as one of the most overpowering winning streaks in sports history.

From 1951–1960, the Canadiens appeared in 10 straight Stanley Cup finals.

The Canadiens have won more NHL championships than any other team.

The Canadiens won four more Stanley Cups in a row from 1976–1979.

Canadiens player Bernie Geoffrion *(left)* slides into the net.

#5 GRETZKY MAKES HISTORY

March 23, 1994 ▪ The Great Western Forum ▪ Inglewood, California

On March 23, 1994, Los Angeles Kings player Wayne Gretzky scored an empty-net goal in the second period against the Vancouver Canucks. But this was not just any goal. It was the 802nd of Gretzky's career! This broke Gordie Howe's all-time scoring record. And Gretzky didn't stop there. He went on to score a career total of 894 goals.

- Gretzky once scored a record 92 goals in a single season.
- At the time of his retirement, Gretzky held 61 NHL records.
- During his career, Gretzky won four Stanley Cups.

Gretzky (#99) shoots his 802nd career goal.

#4 THE BRUINS BOUNCE BACK

May 13, 2013 • TD Garden • Boston, Massachusetts

The Boston Bruins trailed the Toronto Maple Leafs 4–2 with under 90 seconds left in Game 7 of the 2013 Eastern Conference **quarterfinals**. Then, the Bruins made a shocking comeback. They scored 2 goals in just 31 seconds! Bruins center Patrice Bergeron scored the game-tying goal and then the game-winning goal in overtime.

Bergeron had scored only a single goal in the first six games of the series.

The Bruins were the first NHL team to win a Game 7 after trailing by three points in the third period.

The Bruins later made it to the 2013 Stanley Cup finals.

The Bruins give a stick salute to their fans.

The Maple Leafs had previously won two games straight to force a Game 7.

#3 THE GOLDEN GOAL

February 28, 2010 ▪ Canada Hockey Place ▪ Vancouver, British Columbia

Canada led 2–1 against the United States with under a minute left in the 2010 Olympic finals. Suddenly, U.S. player Zach Parise tied the game with 25 seconds left. Almost eight minutes into overtime, Canada's Sidney Crosby shot the puck between the legs of U.S. goalie Ryan Miller! His goal earned Canada their eighth Olympic gold medal in hockey.

Canada has more gold medals in hockey than any other country.

The Canadian team posing with their gold medals

Crosby (#87) gets the puck past two defenders.

In 2014, Crosby and the Canadian team won Olympic gold again!

Crosby tied for the NHL's leading scorer during the 2009–2010 season.

This 2010 game was the most-watched Olympic hockey game in 30 years.

17

#2 THE MIRACLE ON ICE

February 22, 1980 ▪ Lake Placid Arena ▪ Lake Placid, New York

Before the 1980 Olympics, the Soviet Union had won five of the previous six gold medals. The favored Soviets led an inexperienced U.S. team 3–2 in the third period. But then, there was a real surprise—the U.S. scored 2 goals back-to-back for a 4–3 victory! This match was one of the largest upsets in sports history.

The U.S. did not lead in the game until the last 10 minutes.

The U.S. team had the youngest players in the 1980 Olympics.

The U.S. defeated Finland in their next game to win Olympic gold.

The U.S. Olympic players had only played in college or **minor-league** hockey.

This was the first Olympic hockey game the Soviet team had lost since 1968.

19

#1 THE FLYING GOAL

May 10, 1970 ▪ Boston Garden ▪ Boston, Massachusetts

Boston Bruins player Bobby Orr scored one of hockey's greatest goals during Game 4 of the 1970 Stanley Cup finals. The matchup against the St. Louis Blues went into overtime. As Orr scored the game-winning goal, he tripped! The game ended with Orr flying through the air as his team won the championship!

The win was the fourth Stanley Cup victory for the Bruins.

The Bruins with their championship trophy

EVEN MORE EXTREME HOCKEY MOMENTS

In the long history of the NHL, there have been more than 120,000 games. Here are some other exciting moments from hockey history!

THE LONGEST SHOOTOUT
Florida Panthers player Nick Bjugstad ended the longest **shootout** in NHL history against the Washington Capitals on December 16, 2014. The shootout lasted 20 rounds.

JAGR'S SOLO GOAL
The Pittsburgh Penguins trailed the Chicago Blackhawks 4–3 near the end of Game 1 of the 1992 Stanley Cup. Penguins player Jaromir Jagr skated through nearly the entire Blackhawks defense to score a game-tying goal!

BAUN'S BROKEN LEG
Toronto Maple Leafs player Bob Baun broke his leg during Game 6 of the 1964 Stanley Cup against the Detroit Red Wings. But he still came back to score the game-winning goal in overtime!

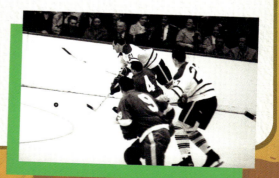

GLOSSARY

center a player who is positioned near the middle of the ice and assists with both offense and defense

empty-net goal a goal scored when there is no goalie guarding the net

even-strength goal a goal scored when both teams have the same number of players on the ice

hat trick when a player scores three goals in one match

minor-league a sports association below the top professional one

penalty shot an opportunity to score at the goal where a player is given no opponent to pass other than the goalie

power-play goal a goal scored when the opponent has fewer players on the ice due to a penalty

quarterfinals the round of playoffs in hockey where the eight remaining teams play to determine the final four teams

shootout a three-round process to break a tie in which each team takes turns shooting at the other's goal

short-handed goal a goal scored when the opponent has more players on the ice than the scoring team

slap shot a play where a player's stick connects with the ice behind the puck, sending the puck flying at a high speed

INDEX

career 9, 13
center 5, 14
championships 6, 8, 12, 20
comebacks 4, 10–11, 14
favorites 7
goalie 7, 11, 16
gold 16–19
NHL 4, 7, 11–13, 15, 17, 21–22
Olympics 18–19
overtime 10, 14, 16, 21–22
players 6–7, 10–13, 16, 19–22
seasons 5–7, 9–11, 13, 17, 21
Stanley Cup 6–10, 12–13, 15, 20, 22
underdogs 11

READ MORE

James, India. *Hockey (The Science Behind the Athlete).* New York: Crabtree Publishing, 2025.

Streeter, Anthony. *Stanley Cup All-Time Greats (All-Time Greats of Sports Championships).* Mendota Heights, MN: Press Box Books, 2025.

LEARN MORE ONLINE

1. Go to **FactSurfer.com** or scan the QR code below.
2. Enter "**10 Hockey Moments**" into the search box.
3. Click on the cover of this book to see a list of websites.

ABOUT THE AUTHOR

Nathan Sommer graduated from the University of Minnesota with degrees in journalism and political science. He lives in Minneapolis, Minnesota, and enjoys camping, hiking, and writing in his free time.